PIECES

BOOKSTACKS

By Robert Creeley

Pieces
Words
The Gold Diggers
The Island
For Love

A Quick Graph
The Charm

PIECES

Robert Creeley

CHARLES SCRIBNER'S SONS · New York

for Louis Zukofsky

Contents

yes, yes,
        that's what
I wanted,
        I always wanted,
I always wanted,
        to return
to the body
        where I was born.

Allen Ginsberg

PIECES

As real as thinking
wonders created
by the possibility—

forms. A period
at the end of a sentence
which

began *it was*
into a present,
a presence

saying
something
as it goes.

   .

No forms less
than activity.

All words—
days—or
eyes—

or happening
is an event only
for the observer?

No one
there. Everyone
here.

   .

Small facts
of eyes, hair
blonde, face

3

looking like a
flat painted
board. How

opaque as if
a reflection
merely, skin

vague glove of
randomly seen
colors.

.

Inside
and out

impossible
locations—

reaching in
from out-

side, out
from in-

side—as
middle:

one
hand.

. . .

4

FLOWERS

No thing less than one thing
or more—

no sun
but sun—

or water
but wetness found—

What truth is it
that makes men so miserable?

Days we die
are particular—

This life cannot be lived
apart from what it must forgive.

.   .   .

THE FAMILY

Father
and mother
and sister
and sister
and sister.

.

Here we are.
There are five
ways to say this.

.   .   .

KATE'S

If I were you
and you were me
I bet you'd
do it too.

.   .   .

FOR YOU

Like watching rings extend in water
this time of life.

.   .   .

A STEP

Things
        come and go.
Then
        let them.

.   .   .

Having to—
what do I think
to say now.

Nothing but
comes and goes
in a moment.

.

Cup.
Bowl.
Saucer.
Full.

.

The way into the form,
the way out of the room—

The door, the hat,
the chair, the fact.

.

Sitting, waves on the beach,
or else clouds, in the sky,

a road, going by,
cars, a truck, animals, in crowds.

. . .

The car
moving
the hill
down

which yellow
leaves
light forms
declare.

.

Car coughing moves with
a jerked energy forward.

.

7

Sit. Eat
a doughnut.

Love's consistency
favors me.

.

A big crow on the
top of the tree's
form more stripped
with leaves gone
overweights it.

. . .

Pieces of cake crumbling
in the hand trying to hold
them together to give each
of the seated guests a piece.

.

Willow, the house, an egg—
what do they make?

Hat, happy, a door—
what more.

. . .

THE FINGER

Either in or out of
the mind, a conception
overrides it. *So that*
that time I was a stranger,

bearded, with clothes that were
old and torn. I was told,
it was known to me, my
fate would be timeless. Again

and again I was to
get it right, the story I
myself knew only the way of,
but the purpose if it

had one, was not mine.
The quiet shatter of the light,
the image folded into
endlessly opening patterns—

had they faced me into
the light so that my
eye was blinded? At moments
I knew they had gone but

searched for her face, the pureness
of its beauty, the endlessly sensual—
but no sense as that now reports it.
Rather, she was beauty, that

Aphrodite I had known of,
and caught sight of as *maid*—
a girlish openness—or known
as a woman turned from the light.

I knew, however, the other,
perhaps even more. She was there
in the room's corner, as she would be,
bent by a wind it seemed

would never stop blowing,
braced like a seabird,

with those endlessly clear grey eyes.
Name her, Athena—what name.

The osprey, the sea, the waves.
To go on telling the story,
to go on though no one hears it,
to the end of my days?

Mercury, Hermes, in dark glasses.
Talk to him—but as if
one talked to the telephone,
telling it to please listen—

is that right, have I said it—
and the reflecting face echoes
some cast of words in mind's eye,
attention a whip of surmise.

And the power to tell
is glory. One unto one
unto one. And though all
mistake it, it is one.

I saw the stones thrown
at her. I felt a radiance transform
my hands and my face.
I blessed her, I was one.

Are there other times?
Is she that woman,
or this one. Am I the man—
and what transforms.

Sit by the fire.
I'll dance a jig I learned
long before we were born
for you and you only then.

I was not to go
as if to somewhere,
was not in the mind
as thinking knows it,

but danced in a jigging
intensive circle
before the fire and its heat
and that woman lounging.

How had she turned herself?
She was largely warm—
flesh heavy—and smiled
in some deepening knowledge.

There are charms.
The pedlar and the small dog
following and the whistled,
insistent song.

I had the pack,
the tattered clothing,
was neither a man nor not one,
all that—

and who was she,
with the fire behind her,
in the mess of that place,
the dust, the scattered pieces,

her skin so warm,
so massive, so stolid in her
smiling the charm did not
move her but rather

kept her half-sleepy attention,
yawning, indulging the manny

who jiggled a world before her
made of his mind.

She was young,
she was old,
she was small.
She was tall with

extraordinary grace. Her face
was all distance, her eyes
the depth of all one had thought of,
again and again and again.

To approach, to hold her,
was not possible.
She laughed and turned
and the heavy folds of cloth

parted. The nakedness
burned. Her heavy breath,
her ugliness, her lust—
but her laughing, her low

chuckling laugh, the way
she moved her hand to the
naked breast, then to
her belly, her hand with its fingers.

Then *shone*—
and whatever is said
in the world, or forgotten,
or not said, makes a form.

The choice is simply,
I will—as mind is a finger,
pointing, as wonder
a place to be.

12

Listen to me, let
me touch you
there. You are young again,
and you are looking at me.

Was there ever
such foolishness more
than what thinks it knows
and cannot see, was there ever

more? Was the truth
behind us, or before?
Was it one
or two, and who was I?

She was laughing, she was
laughing, at me,
and I danced, and
I danced.

Lovely, lovely woman, let
me sing, *one to*
one to one, and let
me follow.

.   .   .

One thing
done, the
rest follows.

.

Not from not
but in in.

.

13

Here here
here. Here.

. . .

I cannot see you
there for what you
thought you were.

The faded memories
myself enclose
passing too.

.

Were you there
or here now—
such a slight sound
what was your step makes.

.

Here I
am. There
you are.

.

The head
of a
pin on . . .

.

Again
and again
now
also.

. . .

GEMINI

Two eyes, two hands—
in one two are given.

The words
are messages

from another,
not understood but given.

.

Neither one, nor the other,
nor of a brother—but in

the one, two, restless,
confined to a place ruled

by a moon, and another one
with messages, rather, sequences

of words that are not to be understood
but somehow given to a world.

All this dances in a room,
two by two, but alone.

.

From one to two,
is the first rule.

Of two minds the twin
is to double life given.

.

What it says is that one
is two, the twin,

that the messenger comes
to either, that these fight

to possess, but do not
understand—that if the

moon rules, there is
"domestic harmony"—but if the blood

cry, the split so divide,
there can be no

company for the two in one.
He is alone.

.   .   .

In secret
the out's in—

the wise
surprised, all

going coming,
begun undone.

Hence the fool dances
in endless happiness.

.

A circling with
snake-tail in mouth—

what the head was
looked *forward*,

what backward is,
then guess.

Either way,
it will stay.

.   .   .

"Time" is some sort of hindsight, or else rhythm of activity
—e.g., now it's 11 days later—"also alive" like they say.

.

Where it is
was and
will be never
only here.

.

—fluttering as
  falling, leaves,
  knives, to
  avoid—tunnel
  down the
  vague sides . . .

.

—it
  it—

.   .   .

"FOLLOW THE DRINKING GOURD . . . "

Present again
present present
again present
present again

leaves falling,
knives, a windspout
of nostalgic faces,
into the air.

Car glides forward.
Drive from Bloomington,
Indiana to Lexington,
Ky. Here the walls

of fall, the stone,
the hill, the trucks
in front with
the unseen drivers.

Stoney Lonesome. Gnaw-
bone. A house
sits back from
the road.

*A Christmas
present—all
present and ac-
counted for? Sir?*

Passage of time.
The sun shone level
from the left-
hand side of

the land—a flat-
seeming distance,
left, east? South?
Sun shines.

*Go on. Tell
me, them, him,*

18

her, their
apparent forms.

The "present dented,"
call it "long
distance," come
here home. Then

a scarecrow there, here a
snowman. Where in
the world then an-
other place?

Drive on
what seems an
exceptionally smooth
and even surface,

the forward cars
way up there glint
in that sun of
a universe of mine.

And for twenty eight
dollars—all this.
All in the mind
in time, in place—

what it costs to rent
agency? Give
me a present, your
hand to help

me understand this.
So far, so long,
so anywhere a
place if not this

one—driving,
screaming a lovely
song perhaps, or
a cigar smoke—

"When they were
young in Kentucky
a man to freedom
took them in a cave . . ."

A famous song,
to drive to,
sing along the
passing way—

or *done* or
right or
wrong or
wander on.

.   .   .

THE MOON

Earlier in the evening the moon
was clear to the east,
over the snow of the yard
and fields—a lovely

bright clarity and perfect
roundness, isolate,
riding as they say the
black sky. Then we went

about our businesses of the
evening, eating supper, talking,

watching television, then
going to bed, making love,

and then to sleep. But before
we did I asked her to look
out the window at the moon
now straight up, so that

she bent her head and looked
sharply up, to see it.
Through the night it must
have shone on, in that

fact of things—another
moon, another night—a
full moon in the winter's
space, a white loneliness.

I came awake to the blue
white light in the darkness,
and felt as if someone
were there, waiting, alone.

. . .

NUMBERS

For Robert Indiana

One

What
singular upright flourishing
condition . . .
it enters here,
it returns here.

.

Who was I that
thought it was
another one by
itself divided or multiplied
produces one.

.

This time, this
place, this
one.

.

You are not
me, nor I you.

.

All ways.

.

As of a stick,
stone, some-

thing so
fixed it has

a head, walks,
talks, leads

a life.

.

Two

When they were
first made, all the

earth must have
been their reflected
bodies, for a moment—
a flood of seeming
bent for a moment back
to the water's glimmering—
how lovely they came.

.

What you wanted
I felt, or felt I felt.
This was more than one.

.

This point of so-called
consciousness is forever
a word making up
this world of more
or less than it is.

.

Don't leave me.
Love me. One by one.

.

As if to sit
by me were another
who did sit. So

to make you
mine, in the mind,
to know you.

.

Three

They come now with
one in the middle—
either side thus
another. Do they

know who each other
is or simply walk
with this pivot between them.
Here forms have possibility.

.

When either this
or that becomes
choice, this fact

of things enters.
What had been
agreed now

alters to
two and one,
all ways.

.

The first
triangle, of form,
of people,

sounded a
lonely occasion I
think—the

circle begins
here, intangible—
yet a birth.

.

Four

This number for me
is comfort, a secure
fact of things. The

table stands on
all fours. The dog
walks comfortably,

and two by two
is not an army
but friends who love

one another. Four
is a square,
or peaceful circle,

celebrating return,
reunion,
love's triumph.

.

The card which is the
four of hearts must
mean enduring experience
of life. What other
meaning could it have.

.

Is a door
four—but
who enters.

.

Abstract—yes, as
two and two
things, four things—
one and three.

.

Five

Two by
two with
now another

in the middle
or else at
the side.

.

From each
of the four
corners draw

a line to
the alternate
points. Where

these intersect
will be
five.

.

When younger this was
a number used to
count with, and

to imagine a useful
group. Somehow the extra
one—what is more than four—

reassured me there would be
enough. Twos and threes or
one and four is plenty.

        .

A way to draw stars.

        .

Six
——

Twisting
        as forms of it
two and three—

        on the sixth
day had finished
        all creation—

hence holy—
        or that the sun
is "furthest from

        equator & appears
to pause, before
        returning . . ."

or that it "contains
        the first even number
(2), and the first odd

27

number (3), the former representing
the male member, and the latter
    the *muliebris pudenda* . . ."

Or two triangles interlocked.

.

Seven

We are seven, echoes in
my head like a nightmare of
responsibility—seven
days in the week, seven
years for the itch of
unequivocal involvement.

.

Look
at
the
light
of
this
hour.

.

I was born at seven in
the morning and my
father had a monument
of stone, a pillar, put
at the entrance of the
hospital, of which he was head.

.

*At sixes
and sevens*—the pen
lost, the paper:

a night's dead
drunkenness. Why
the death of something now

so near if *this*
number is holy.
Are all

numbers one?
Is counting forever
beginning again.

.

Let this be the end of the seven.

.

Eight

Say "eight"—
be patient.

Two fours
show the way.

.

Only this number
marks the cycle—

the eight year interval—
for that confluence

makes the full moon shine
on the longest

or shortest
day of the year.

.

Now summer fades.
August its month—
this interval.

.

She is eight
years old, holds
a kitten, and
looks out at me.

.

Where are you.
One table.
One chair.

.

In light lines count the interval.
Eight makes the time wait quietly.

.

No going back—
though half is
four and
half again
is two.

.

Oct-
ag-
on-
al.

     •

Nine

There is no point
of rest here.
It wavers,

it reflects multiply
the *three*
times three.

Like a mirror
it returns here
by being there.

     •

Perhaps in the
emphasis implicit—
over and over—

"triad of triads,"
"triply sacred and perfect
number"—that

resolves what—
in the shifting,
fading containment?

     •

Somehow the game
where a nutshell covers
the one object, a

stone or coin, and
the hand is
quicker than the eye—

how is that *nine*,
and not *three*
chances, except that

three imaginations of it
might be, and there are
two who play—

making six, but
the world is real also,
in itself.

.

More. The nine months
of waiting that discover
life or death—

another life or death—
not yours, not
mine, as we watch.

.

The serial diminish-
ment or progression of
the products which

helped me remember:
nine times two is one-eight
            nine times nine is eight-one—
at each end,

move forward, backward,
then, and the same
numbers will occur.

        .

What law
or
mystery

is involved
protects
itself.

        .

Zero

Where are you—who
        by not being here
are here, but here
        by not being here?

There is no trick to reality—
        a mind
makes it, any
        mind. You

walk the years in a
        nothing, a no
place I know as well as
        the last breath

I took, blowing the smoke
    out of a mouth
will also go nowhere,
      having found its way.

.

Reading that primitive systems
seem to have natural cause for
the return to one, after ten—
but this is *not* ten—out of
nothing, one, to return to that—
Americans have a funny way—
somebody wrote a poem about it—
of "doing nothing"—What else
should, *can*, they do?

.

What
by being not
is—is not
by being.

.

When holes taste good
we'll put them in our bread

.

The Fool

    "With light step, as if earth and its trammels had little power to restrain him, a young man in gorgeous vestments pauses at the brink of a precipice among the great heights of the world; he surveys the blue distance before him—its expanse of sky rather than the prospect below. His act of eager walking is still indicated, though he is stationary at the given moment; his dog is still bounding. The edge which opens on the depth has no terror; it is as if angels were waiting to uphold him, if it came about that he leaped from the height. His countenance is full of intelligence and expectant dream. He has a rose in one hand and in the other a costly wand, from which depends over his right shoulder a wallet curiously embroidered. He is a prince of the other world on his travels through this one—all amidst the morning glory, in the keen air. The sun, which shines behind him, knows whence he came, whither he is going, and how he will return by another path after many days . . ."

.   .   .

The bedpost is an
extraordinary shape
to have happened though
in nature this upthrust

with its conical cap and
bulging middle is met
with often enough. But the
bar, horizontal, joining

the two posts, I have not
seen this elsewhere except
as the cross bar of the collar
bone, my own, or those of others.

.

What she says she wants
she wants she says.

.   .   .

One/ the Sun/
Moon/ one.

.

How far one has come
in these seven league boots.

.

The pen,
the lines it
leaves, forms
divine—nor
laugh nor giggle.
This prescription
is true.
Truth is a scrawl,
all told
in all.

.

Back where things were
sweeter, water falls
and thinks again.

.

Here, there,
every-
where.

.

Never write
to say more

than saying
something.

Words
are
pleasure.
All
words.

.

NAMES

Harry has written
all he knows.
Miriam tells
her thought, Peter
says again
his mind. Robert and John,
William, Tom,
and Helen, Ethel,
that woman whose name
he can't remember
or she even him
says to tell
all they know.

.   .   .

Can feel it in the pushing,
not letting myself relax
for any reason, hanging on.

.

Thinking—and coincident
experience of the situation.

"I think he'll hit me."
He does. Etc.

.

Reflector/ -ive/ -ed.

.

CHICAGO

Say that you're
        lonely—and want
something to
        place you—

going around groping
        either by mind
or hand—but behind
        the pun is a

door you keep open,
        one way,
so they won't touch you
        and still let you stay.

.

I can't see in
        this place more
than the walls
        and door—
a light flat
        and air hot,
and drab, drab, drab
        and locked.

Would dying be here?
Never go anywhere you
        can't live.

Concrete blocks painted an "off white" yellow tone—in-stitutional—*very* noisy, senses of people next side of wall, etc. Get *used* to shrinking space— They'll let you out when there's reason.

.   .   .

Pleasures of pain,
        oh lady,
fail in the argument—
        This way

of making friends
        you made me let
go of, losing myself
        in a simple fact.

        .

NYC—

    Streets as ever blocky, grey—square sense of rectangu-lar enclosures, emphasized by the coldness of the time of year, and the rain. In moving in the cab—continual sense of small (as size, i.e., all "cars," etc.) persistent diffi-culties.

        .

THE FRIENDS

I want to help you
by understanding what
you want me to
understand by saying so.

    .

I listen. I had
an ego once upon
a time—I do still,
for you listen to me.

Let's be very still.
Do you hear? Hear
what, I will say when-
ever you ask me to listen.

    .

I wouldn't joke about
your wife wanting to wash
her hair at eleven o'clock
at night but supposing she

wants to I'd consider her
thoughts on the matter equally
with yours wherever you were
and for whatever reason.

    .

Don't think I'm
so awful you can
afford my company
so as not to
put me down more.

    .

God, I hate
simplistic logic like—
I like it. Who cares.

   .

Liking is as
liking does
for you, for me.

   .

The "breathtaking banalities"
one only accomplishes in
retrospect. Hindsight—

they call it—like the
backend of a horse. *Horse's
ass*, would be the way.

  . . .

DICTION

The grand time when the words
were fit for human allegation,

and imagination of small, local
containments, and the lids fit.

What was the wind blew through it,
a veritable bonfire like they say—

and did say in hostile, little voices:
"It's changed, it's not the same!"

   .

AMERICA

America, you ode for reality!
Give back the people you took.

Let the sun shine again
on the four corners of the world

you thought of first but do not
own, or keep like a convenience.

People are your own word, you
invented that locus and term.

Here, you said and say, is
where we are. Give back

what we are, these people you made,
us, and nowhere but you to be.

.

CITIZEN

Write a giggly ode about
        motherfuckers—Oedipus—
or Lysergic Acid—a word
        for an experience, verb

or noun. Count down, count
        Orlovsky, count up—
in the air, you filthy
        window washer. Why

not clean up the world.
        You need it, I
need it—more than
        either one of us can get.

.

PLACE

Thinking of you asleep on a
      bed on a pillow, on a
      bed—the ground or space

you lie on. That's enough to
      talk to now I got space and
      time like a broken watch.

.

Hello there—instant
reality on the other
end of this so-called line.

.

Oh no you
don't, do you?

.

Late, the words, late
the form of them, al-

ready past what they were
fit for, one and two and three.

.

THE PURITAN ETHOS

Happy the man who loves what
he has and worked for it also.

.

There is a lake of clear water.
There are forms of things despite us.

43

Pope said, "a little learning,"
and, and, and, and—the same.

Why don't you go home and sleep
and come back and talk some more.

.

By location, e.g., where
or here—or what words in
time make of things. *Space,*
they say, and think a several

dimensioned locus. Mr.
Warner came from a small
town in the middle mid-
eastern Atlantic states.

That—in time—displaces
all else might be said of
him, or whatever became
of him in that other space he knew.

.

THE PROVINCE

Trying to get "our men
back" and "our ship
back"—"tactical
nuclear weapons"—dig!

Shee-it. The *world,*
dad, is where you
live unless you've for-
gotten it through that

incredible means called
     efficacy *or* understanding
or superior lines of
     or, or something else.

   .

CANADA

"The maple leaf forever"
    "in 1867—"
"inspired the world
    to say—"

  .   .   .

Happy love, this
agreement, coincidence
like crossing streets.

   .

Forms face
facts find.

   .

One cock
pheasant one
hen pheasant
walk along.

  .   .   .

THE BOY

Push yourself in on others
hard enough, they beat you
with sticks and whips—the birth

of love. E.g., affection aroused,
it moves to be close, touch, and
feel the warm livingness of an-

other, any other, sucked, stroked,
the club itself possibly a symbol of
the obvious. My mother had hair,

and when I grew older, so did
I, all over my face, which I wanted
to be there, and grew a beard henceforth.

.   .   .

3 IN 1

for Charlotte

The bird
flies
out the
window. She
flies.

.

The bird flies
out the
window. She
flies.

.

46

The bird
flies. She
flies.

. . .

THEY

What could
they give me I
hadn't myself
discovered—

The *world*,—that
I'd fallen upon
in some
distracted drunkenness—

Or that the rules
were *wrong*, an
observation they
as well as I
knew now—

They were imagination
also. If they
would be as the
mind could see *them*,

then it all was
true and the
mind followed and
I also.

.

47

ECHO

Yes but your sweetness
derives drunkenness—

over, and over, not
your face, not your

hand—no you nor
me is real now—

Nothing here now,
nothing there now.

    .

In this fact of face and body—looking out—a *kind* of
pleasure. That is, no argument stops me. Not—"yes"—
"no"—gradually? Only involved as openings, sexual also,
seem to be—but is "no" my final way of speaking? E.g.,
a "poet" of such impossibilities "I" makes up?

  . . .

So tired
it falls
apart.

  . . .

Why say to them
truth is confounded with opposition,
or that—*or that* what is
were a happiness.

Simple, to be said, a life
is nothing more than itself,

and all the bodies together
are, one by one, the measure.

      .

I am finally
what I had to be,
neither more nor less—
become happiness.

   .   .   .

Forms' passage as
water beside the white
upright group of apparently
flat buildings— The river's
bend, seen from the sky—
down, under, with the eye.

      .

Allen's saying as we fly out of NYC—the look of the city
underneath us like a cellular growth, "cancer"—so that
senses of men on the earth as an investment of it radiates
a world cancer—Burroughs' "law" finally quite clear.

      .

Mississippi much as—pen blots with pressure (?)—the sky
ahead a faint light yellow—like "northern" lights. —Why
the goddamn impatience with that AS—the damn function
of *simile*, always a displacement of what *is* happening.

      .

Life like you
think you have
it till it isn't

—but is, inevitably—
behind the scene.

.   .   .

Days later—neither having
become nor not become a
convenience to assumptions.

.

You look up the street to
the far bay and boats
floating in a sunny haze.

Either way, the streets lead
down, from this hill. An
apartment house of tiered

layers sits opposite on
the far corner. We get
into the car and drive off.

.

Nowhere one
goes will
one ever
be away
enough from
wherever
one was.

.

Falling-in windows—
the greenhouse back of

50

Curleys' house. The
Curleys were so good
to me, their mother
held me on her lap.

. . .

No clouds out the window,
flat faint sky of faded blue.
The sun makes spring now,

a renewal possibly of like energy,
something forgotten almost remembered,
echoes in my mind like the grass.

.

Your opaqueness, at moments,
would be the mirror. Your
face closed as a door—

that insists on nothing,
but not to be entered—
wanting simply to be left alone.

I slept, it seemed, the moment
I lay down in the bed, even,
it might have been, impatient

to be out of it, gone away,
to what densities can be there
in a night's sleep, day by day.

But, all in the mind it comes
and goes. My own life is given
me back again, something forgotten.

.

I want to sing.
What makes it
impossible—so

that one lifts
that dead bulk
with such insistent energy?

.

"But now it's come to distances . . ."
—Leonard Cohen

.

Thinking—a tacit, tactile distance between us at this
moment—much as if we had lives in "different worlds"—
which, I suppose, would be the case despite all closeness
otherwise, i.e., almost as if the moment one were "thinking,"
and not literally taking, finding place in something we both
had occasion in, that this fact of things becomes a separa-
tion. I.e., it seems not possible to live the "same" life, no
matter what one wants, wills, or tries to have the so-called
"case."—Like old "romantic" self-query, come of obvious
unrest and frustration.

.   .   .

ECHO OF

Can't myself
let off this
fiction. "You
don't exist,

baby, you're
dead." Walk

52

off, on—the
light bulb

overhead, beside,
or, the bed, you
think you laid
on? When, what.

.

THE

The water
waiting far
off to the
east, the
west—the
shores of the world.

.   .   .

Situation of feeling increasingly "apart" from people in
reading—and/or probably the fact of going *into* the reading
to find a place in the welter of randomness of people there
—*or* my assumption, in fatigue, that no one's making it.

.

You are all lovely,
hairy, scarey
people after all.

.

AGAIN

One more day gone,
done, found in
the form of days.

It began, it
ended—was
forward, backward,

slow, fast, a
sun shone, clouds,
high in the air I was

for awhile with others,
then came down
on the ground again.

No moon. A room in
a hotel—to begin
again.

. . .

The which it
was, form
seen—there
here, re-
peated for/
as/—There
is a "parallel."

.

When and/or if, as,—however, you do "speak" to people,
i.e., as condition of the circumstance (as Latin: "what's
around") a/n "im(in)pression." "I'll" *crush* you to "death"—
"flying home."

.

Allen last night—context of *how* include the output of human function in an experience thereof makes the fact of it become possibility of pleasure—not fear, not pain. Everybody *spends* it (the "life" they inhabit) all—hence, no problem of that kind, except (*large* fact) in imagination.

.   .   .

In the house of
old friend, whose
friend, my

friend, the trouble
with you, who,
he is, there, here,
we were *not*.

.

The voice of the
echo of time, the
same—"I

know you," no
pain in that, we are
all around what we are.

.

(Re Bob's film, CUT)

Pictures of the movement.
Pictures of the red-headed
man going down on—

pictures of the red-
haired man on the red-
headed girl on the—

pictures of the flat form
cutting hair off, the long,
the echoic scissors cutting.

.

—Like problem of depth perception, each movement to the
familiarity (a 20 year "distance") confronts the time—as—
distance of the "real" event, i.e., *now*—but "here," as a
habit, is what we are lacking *here*.

.   .   .

P.S.

Thinking of Olson—"we are
as we find out we are."

.   .   .

ICE CREAM

Sure,
Herbert—
Take a bite—

The crowd
milling on the bridge, the
night forms in

the air. So
much has gone
away.

.

56

Upside
down
forms
faces.

.

Letter to General
Eisenhower from

General
Mount-

batten.
Better

be
right.

Better batter
bigger pancakes.

You Chief
Eat It.

.

Something that hasn't as yet had chance to
wants the possibility of asking

if what might be might be,
if what has to be is otherwise.

.

Oh so cute in your
gorgeous gown you were.

*You were, you were,
you-are-or-you-were-you-were.*

.   .   .

What
do you think it is.
Dogs wandering
the roads.

All I knew or know
began with this—
emptiness
with its incessant movement.

Where was it—
to be younger, older,
if not here,
if not there.

Calling,
calling over the shoulder,
through a mist,
to those fading people.

.

This singleness
you make an evidence
has purpose.

You are not alone,
however one—not
so alone.

Light finds a place
you can see it in
such singleness.

.

There might be
an imaginary

place to be—
there might be.

.

Grey mist forms
out the window,
leaves showing green,
the dark trunks of trees—

place beyond?
The eye sees, the
head apparently records
the vision of these eyes.

What have I seen,
now see? There were
times before
I look now.

.

Re C—

Making a form for you
of something, a vehicle
of the head, round
wheel eyes for getting there.

Why do you get up so
restlessly if sitting down is
where I always find you—
after all these years.

You want to fight?
You want a black eye for
your troubles? How be
young and yet to be loved?

Sprightly, you have a
head I do put wheels on,
and two arms and two legs.
You'll travel.

.   .   .

Like a man committed to searching
out long darkened corridors with doors,
and only the spot of the flashlight to
be a way into and back out, to safety.

.

Peace, brother, to all of it,
in all senses, in all places,
in every way, in all
senses, in all places, in
every way.

.

Here now *you* are—
by what means?
And who to know it?

.

A lady in a dress of velvet,
a girl in a cotton dress,
a woman, walking—
something like that, with hair—

some form you feel or
you said you felt was
like that the times we sat
and you told me what

to look for—this
fact of some woman
with some man like
that was really all.

.

The sun will set again on
the edge of the sky or whatever

you want to call it. *Out there,*
not here, the sun "will set,

did set, is *now* setting."
Hear, goddamnit, hear.

.

I have no ease
calling things beautiful
which are by that
so called to my mind.

.

You want

the fact

of things

in words,

of words.

.

Endless trouble, endless pleasure,
endless distance, endless ways.

.

What do you want with the phone
if you won't answer it.

.

Don't say it doesn't rhyme
if you won't read it—nor break the

line in pieces that goes
and goes and goes.

.

Each moment constitutes reality,
or rather may constitute
reality, or may have *done*
so, or perhaps *will?*

I'd rather sit on my
hands on purpose, and be
an idiot—or just go off somewhere,
like they say, to something else.

.

THE NEWS

Unresponsible
people versus

serious
people. In

New Brunswick
this is a problem.

*

The language
of instruction
for their children . . .

    *

The English
speaking people
are not
a numerous group . . .

    *

Allentown
Arts Festival
Days . . .

late
film and
video tape
report . . .

    *

NIAGARA MOHAWK

. . .

Smell of gum wrappers as of Saturday afternoon at movies
in Maynard, Mass.—

Sudden openness of summer—everything seems to hang in
the air.

.

I figure

if I eat so much,
I get so fat.

If I don't eat so much
I don't get so fat—

so,
so.

.

Laugh at the domestic comedy,
the woman falls flat on her face,

the man staggers down the street,
the kid falls down, the dog dies.

Think of the implications,
what you could sell.

.

"It's rare that the city of Buffalo
gets to shape its own destiny . . ."

.

Take advantage of this,
take advantage of what's downtown
and link the two with a
rapid transit system . . .

. . .

Where we are there must
be something to place us.

Look around. What do you see
that you can recognize.

.

Anxious about the weather,
folding the door shut, unwrapping
the floor covering and rolling it
forward, at the door.

.

So that's what you do:
ask the same question
and keep answering.

.

Was that right.

.   .   .

The day comes and goes,
the far vistas of the west
are piles of clouds and
an impending storm. I see
it all now—nothing more.

.

Love in a
car takes my
wife away from me.

She is busy. She thinks
in an activity and goes
about her own business.

.

Love one.
Kiss two.

    .

In my own ego structure, have to find *place* for shift in imagination of experience—or else—more probably—walk as ever, even sentimentally, straight ahead. In age of hanging gardens variety, now,—all possible, either way— and times insist on "no problems." That way, so to speak, there never was.—One wants *one*.

"Love,
Bob"

. . .

The first
time is
the first
time. The
second
time think
again.

  .

There you
were,
all
the time.

  .

I can
not give
it back.

  .

Your was there
here in any
way you
were.

. . .

MAZATLAN: SEA

The sea flat out,
the light far out,
sky red, the
blobs of dark clouds
seem closer, beyond
the far lateral of
extended sea.

.

Shimmer of reflected
sand tones, the flat
ripples as the water
moves back—an oscil-
lation, endlessly in-
stinct movement—leaves
a ribbing after itself
it then returns to.

.

Bird flicker, light
sharp, flat—the
green hills of the two
islands make a familiar
measure, momently seen.

.

67

The air is thick
and wet and
comfortably encloses
with the sea's sounds.

.

Sleep—it washes
away.

.   .   .

Kids walking beach,
minnow pools—
who knows which.

.

Nothing grand—
The scale is neither
big nor small.

.

Want to get the sense of "I" into Zukofsky's "eye"—a
locus of experience, not a presumption of expected value.

.

Here now—
begin!

.   .   .

B—

Crazy kid-face
skun, in water—

wide hips. The white,
white skin—a big
eared almost feral
toothed woman—
lovely in all particulars.

.

Other way—dark
eyed, the face a
glow of some other
experience, deepens
in the air.

.   .   .

Agh—man
thinks.

.

Moving away in time,
as they say: *days
later*. Later than this—
what swings in the day's
particulars, one to one.

.

An unexamined hump
at first of no
interest lifting out
of the beach at
last devoured us all.

.

Sell the motherfucker for
several hundred dollars.

.

". . . I ran out of my cabin, both glad and frightened,
shouting, 'A noble earthquake! A noble earthquake!' feeling sure I was going to learn something." [John Muir, *The
Yosemite*, p. 59.]

. . .

The kick
of the foot against . . .

.

Make time
of irritations,
looking for the
recurrence—

waiting, waiting,
on the edge of its
to be there
where it was, waiting.

.

Moving in the mind's
patterns, recognized
because there is where
they happen.

.

Grease
on the hands—

. . .

FOUR

Before I die.
Before I die.
Before I die.
Before I die.

. . .

How that fact of
seeing someone you love away
from you in time will
disappear in time, too.

.

Here is all there is,
but *there* seems so
insistently across the way.

.

Heal it, be
patient with
it—be quiet.

.

Across the
table,
years.

. . .

HERE

Past time—those
memories opened
places and minds,
things of such reassurance—

now the twist,
and what was a road
turns to a circle
with nothing behind.

   .

I didn't know what I could do.
I have never known it
but in doing found it
as best I could.

Here I am still,
waiting for that discovery.
What morning, what way now,
will be its token.

   .

They all walk by
on the beach,
large, or little,
crippled, on the face
of the earth.

   .

The wind holds
my leg like

a warm hand.

   . . .

Some nights, a fearful
waking—beside me
you were sleeping,
what your body was

a quiet, apparent
containment. All the world is
this tension, you or me,
seen in that mirror,

patent, pathetic, insured.
I grow bored with lives
of such orders—my own
the least if even yours the most.

                    .

No one lives in
the life of another—
no one knows.

In the singular
the many cohere,
but not to know it.

Here, here, the body
screaming its orders,
learns of its own.

                    .

What would you have
of the princess—
large ears, to hear?
Hands with soft fingers?

You will ride away
into the forest, you will

meet her there
but you will know her.

Why not another
not expected, some
lovely presence suddenly
declared?

All in your mind
the body is, and of
the body such
you make her.

.

One, two,
is the rule—

from there to three
simple enough.

Now four
makes the door

back again
to one and one.

.

My plan is
these little boxes
make sequences . . .

.

Lift me
from such I
makes such declaration.

.

74

Hearing it—*snivelling*—
wanting the reassurance of
another's decision.

There is no one precedes—
look ahead—and behind
you have only where you were.

. . .

You see the jerked
movement, in the
rigid frame, the
boy—the tense stricken

animal, and behind,
the sea moves and
relaxes. The island sits
in its immovable comfort.

What, in the head, goes wrong—
the circuit suddenly
charged with contraries,
and time only is left.

.

The sun drops. The swimmers
grow black in the silver
glitter. The water slurs
and recurs. The air is soft.

. . .

Could write of fucking—
rather its instant or the slow
longing at times of its approach—

how the young man desires,
how, older, it is never known
but, familiar, comes to be so.

How your breasts, love,
fall in a rhythm also familiar,
neither tired nor so young they

push forward. I hate the metaphors.
I want you. I am still alone,
but want you with me.

.   .   .

Listless,
the heat rises—
the whole beach

vacant,
sluggish.
The forms shift

before we know,
before we thought
to know it.

The mind
again, the manner
of mind in the

body, the
weather, the waves,
the sun grows lower

in the faded
sky. Washed
out—the afternoon

of another day
with other people,
looking out of other eyes.

Only the
children, the sea,
the slight wind move

with the
same insistent
particularity.

        .

I was sleeping
and saw the context
of people, dense
around me, talked
into their forms, almost

strident. There were
bright colors, intense
voices. We were, like
they say, discussing

some point of procedure—
would they go, or
come—and waking,
no one but my wife there,
the room faint, bare.

        .

"It's strange. It's
all fallen
to grey."

.

How much
money is
there now?

Count it
again. There's
enough.

.

What changes.
Is the weather
all there is.

.   .   .

Such strangeness of mind I know
I cannot find there more
than what I know.

I am tired of purposes,
intent that leads itself
back to its own belief. I want

nothing more of such brilliance
but what makes the shadows darker
and that fire grow dimmer.

.

Counting age as form
I feel the mark of one
who has been born and grown
to a little past return.

The body will not go
apart from itself to be
another possibility.
It lives where it finds home.

Thinking to alter all
I looked first to myself,
but have learned the foolishness
that wants an altered form.

Here now I am at best,
or what I think I am
must follow as the rest
and live the best it can.

.

There was no one there.
Rather I thought I saw her,
and named her beauty.

For that time we lived
all in my mind
with what time gives.

The substance of one
is not two. No thought
can ever come to that.

I could fashion another
were I to lose her.
Such is thought.

.

Why the echo of
the old music
haunting all? Why

the lift and fall
of the old rhythms,
and aches and pains.

Why one, why two,
why not go utterly
away from all of it.

.

Last night's dream of a complex of people, almost suburban
it seemed, with plots to uncover like a thriller. One moment as we walk to some house through the dark, a man
suddenly appears behind us who throws himself at us, arms
reaching out, but falls short and lands, skids, spread-eagled
on the sidewalk. Then later, in another dream, we are bring-
ing beer somewhere on a sort of truck, rather the cab of
one, nothing back of it, and I am hanging on the side which
I realize is little more than a scaffolding—and the wheels
nearly brush me in turning. Then, much later, I hear our
dog yelp—three times it now seems—so vividly I'm awake
and thinking he must be outside the door of this room
though he is literally in another country. Reading Yeats:
"May we not learn some day to rewrite our histories, when
they touch upon these things?"

. . .

When he and I,
after drinking and
talking, approached
the goddess or woman

become her, and by my
insistence entered
her, and in the ease
and delight of the

meeting I was given that
sight gave me myself,
this was the mystery
I had come to—all

manner of men, a
throng, and bodies of
women, writhing, and
a great though seemingly

silent sound—and when
I left the room to them,
I felt, as though hearing
laughter, my own heart lighten.

.

What do you do,
what do you say,
what do you think,
what do you know.